*Welcome to Korea,*
*where the past is always present,*
*and traditions inspire the future.*

◀ Cover image: *Mirror*
Bronze, 16.5 cm
Goryeo
Loaned by Dr. Chester and Mrs. Wanda Chang
See Pages 56, 58

◀ *Carving of tiger with two human figures*
Antler, green dye, 7 cm
Undated (collected in 1890s)
Collected by Commodore Robert Shufeldt
Smithsonian, Dept. of Anthropology, E211173
See Page 34

▶ *Korea Gallery Entrance*
Korea's past is present for museum visitors beginning their tour of the Korea Gallery from
either of two entrances. From this entrance, visitors see 21st-century Korean wedding clothing
for bride and groom by designer Lee Young Hee, inspired by Joseon dynasty patterns (left), a
hand-carved wooden *sotdae* by Northern Virginia sculptor Sam-kyun Yoon (center), and two
19th-century stone tomb guardians from Korea's Gyeonggi province (right).

▶ *Smithsonian's National Museum of Natural History*
A banner (at left) outside the Smithsonian's National Museum of Natural History Mall
entrance (June 12, 2007) highlights the new Korea Gallery exhibition, which opened to the
public on June 8th.

# FLAGSHIP OF A FLEET
## A Korea Gallery Guide

# FLAGSHIP OF A FLEET
## A Korea Gallery Guide

Paul Michael Taylor
Christopher Lotis

Asian Cultural History Program
National Museum of Natural History
Smithsonian Institution

This book has been made possible by the generous financial assistance of **GK Power,** with special thanks to: **Mr. Seo Kyoung-duk** and **Mr. Hyek Chen.** Design services donated by: **KI Graphics.**

This book is produced and distributed by:
Asian Cultural History Program
Department of Anthropology
Smithsonian Institution
Washington DC 20560-0112 USA

ISBN: 978-0-9724557-0-1
First edition. First printing.

Cataloging-in-Publication Data

Taylor, Paul Michael, 1953-
   **Flagship of a fleet : a Korea Gallery guide** / by Paul Michael Taylor and Christopher Lotis.
   — 1st ed. 116 p. ; 23 cm.
   ISBN-10: 0972455701 — ISBN-13: 978-09724557-0-1
   1. National Museum of Natural History (U.S.)—Guidebooks. 2. Arts, Korean—Washington
   (D.C.)—Guidebooks. 3. National Museum of Natural History (U.S.) Asian Cultural History
   Program I. Lotis, Christopher J. (Christopher Josef), 1977- II. Title. NX584.6.A1T39 2008

Photography content and preliminary design coordination by Dong-Hyok So.
Portions of text are taken from P.M. Taylor's "Introduction" to C.S. Houchins (2004) *An Ethnography of the Hermit Kingdom: The J. B. Bernadou Korean Collection 1884-1885* (Washington, D.C.: Smithsonian, Asian Cultural History Program); and from the Korea Gallery exhibition script (see Acknowledgements).

Book Design by Sooki Moon, KI Graphics, with the help of Erin Byun.

Published in conjunction with the Korea Gallery, an exhibition co-curated by Paul Michael Taylor and Chang-su Cho Houchins (Asian Cultural History Program, National Museum of Natural History, Smithsonian Institution).

The Korea Gallery was made possible by the generous sponsorship of The Korea Foundation, with additional support from GK Power and Korean Air, and from many other donors and sponsors, including: Byun, Joung-hun, Pung Yoon (Minn) Chang, Gangjin City (Korea), Gwangju City (Korea), Jeonju City (Korea), KI Graphics, Mookjae Kwon Myoung-won, Lee Young Hee Museum, LG Electronics, Brian and Moon O'Connor, Yong In University, Sam-kyun Yoon.

Special thanks also to the Embassy of the Republic of Korea (Washington, D.C.) and to the National Folk Museum of Korea; and special thanks for community support to the Korean Heritage Foundation (Arlington, Virginia).

Authors' notes:
**Measurements** for objects in the Korea Gallery are given in centimeters. Unless otherwise noted, a single measurement indicates diameter or maximum dimension (height or length); otherwise the information on the dimensions is ordered as follows: height by width by depth.
**Korean names** in the Gallery use the current standard transcription with the family name first, except for those Koreans who choose other ways of writing their names. Korean Americans, for example, often write their family name last.

*Tomb guardians (Muninseok)*
Granite, 113 x 39 x 30 cm (left, measured from the top of the base)
109 x 40 x 32 cm (right, measured from the top of the base)
19th century
Gyeonggi province, Korea
Loan from Sejoong Stone Museum

Dressed in traditional scholar's hats and robes, these tombs guardians once
protected an ancestral tomb from evil spirits. The practice of placing tomb
guardians near a gravesite dates back about one thousand years.

***Flask with flower design***
Stoneware, *buncheong* ware, 21 x 19 x 12 cm
15th–16th century, Joseon
Smithsonian, Dept. of Anthropology, E409150
See Page 66

# CONTENTS

Ginseng: A Billion Dollar Industry
Called the "elixir of life" and "king of the herbs," Korean ginseng is nearly extinct in its native mountainous habitat. But the plant has been cultivated for centuries, and it is now raised on large farms and exported around the world as a health supplement.

*The Korea Gallery at the Smithsonian's National Museum of Natural History*

한글은 한국문화의 자랑

# HANGEUL: SYMBOL OF PRIDE

**The invention of a syllabic writing system for the Korean language is a significant achievement for Korean scholarship.**

Called *hangeul*, (pronounced HAHN-guhl), the script dates back to the 15th century when King Sejong, with the help of scholars, invented a new writing system based on the sounds of the spoken language. *Hangeul* was used for informal genres like household manuals, Buddhist texts, and light fiction.

But for centuries after its invention, formal documents and scholarly works used Chinese characters to write Korean words. The first *hangeul* newspapers appeared in the late 1800s.

King Sejong (?? 1397–1450)

*Create Hangeul words now!*

*Building hangeul words*

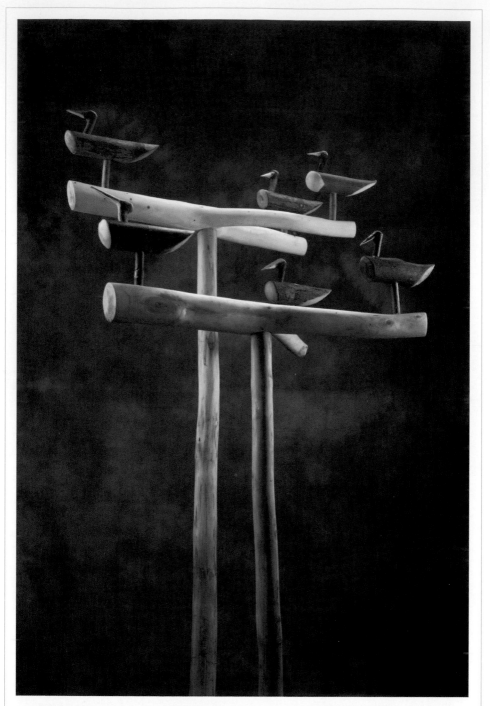

**Sotdae**
Pine, 365 cm
2007
By Sam-kyun Yoon

Erecting *sotdae* (pronounced SOHT-day) at the entrance to a village or by an ancestral grave is a very old Korean tradition still practiced today. These carved ducks atop tall wooden poles guard against the three calamities—flood, fire, and windstorm and three disasters—war, pestilence, and famine.

# FLAGSHIP OF A FLEET

*This book presents the Korea Gallery, at the Smithsonian's National Museum of Natural History, as one of many manifestations of a long history of dialog and exchanges between Korea and the Smithsonian Institution, America's national museum system.*

Any exhibition is the product of a particular time and place, even when (as in this case) the exhibition attempts to portray, in a space of very modest size and for a huge audience (including many people unfamiliar with the topic), a few selected aspects of the vast legacy of the cultural history of an entire people. The identity of the Korean people as a unitary culture speaking one language also developed in a particular place, thousands of years ago on a peninsula of East Asia. The landscapes, geography, fauna and flora of that peninsula, Korea, are of particular interest and importance to audiences visiting a natural history museum with a cultural history component (as is the norm in American natural history museums, unlike those of many other countries including Korea, where natural and cultural history are more often found in separate museums). Although influenced by other Asian cultures in the past and by globalization today, Korea retains many of its unique traditions and a strong national identity. Wherever people of Korean heritage live, they feel a strong connection to their ancestral land – its ancient past and its dynamic present.

This book presents the Korea Gallery, at the Smithsonian's National Museum of Natural History, as one of many

A Korea Gallery banner hangs from the entrance
of the Smithsonian's National Museum of Natural
History, June 2007.

Emissaries of Peace
The 1762 Cherokee & British Delegations

JUNE 27, 2007 – NOVEMBER 25, 2007

manifestations of a long history of dialog and exchanges between Korea and the Smithsonian Institution, America's national museum system. Like the exhibition itself, this book attempts to introduce Korea to a broad audience. For those who have viewed the exhibition (at least in its opening year, since we hope for continuing enhancements and changes over time), it serves as a reminder of the exhibition's themes and of many memorable objects displayed there. It also serves as a proxy in printed form for many people who are unable to visit Washington to view the exhibition. This book presents the first published photographs and descriptions of many previously unpublished Korean artifacts and artworks, adding new information to the rapidly developing literature on the art and material culture of Korea. The object descriptions draw heavily on exhibition text produced by all members of the Korea Gallery development team (see Acknowledgements). Finally, consistent with the growing recent interest in museums themselves, as subjects of study and interpretation, this introduction attempts to provide some background on how this exhibition fits within a range of other ways the Smithsonian, and particularly the Asian Cultural History Program of the National Museum of Natural History, has approached the collection and representation of Korean heritage. We consider the exhibition to be a "flagship" of a fleet of related activities in the field of Korean heritage, including research, education, outreach, public programs and the development and improvement of museum collections.

## Past is Present in 21st-Century Korea

Representing a land with thousands of years of history, the objects in the Korea Gallery cover a broad range of time periods – from the stone "semi-lunar knife" (used to gather rice) made in the 5th or 6th century B.C., to the magnificent modern bride and groom wedding costume set (which draws on ancient Korean patterns and symbols) made in 2006 by contemporary Korean designer Lee Young Hee. A section on Korea's ceramics, drawn mostly from the Museum's collection, represents the depth and richness of Korea's cultural legacy. The oldest ceramics in the exhibition come from the tombs of rulers buried 1,500 years ago; the most recent are from the twenty-first century.

The exhibition includes calligraphy, wooden furniture, stone and wooden sculptures, and paintings. Thematic sections of the Korea Gallery include: "Korean Ceramics: A Tradition of Excellence"; "Honoring Family"; "The Korean Wedding"; "Hangeul: Symbol of Pride" (about calligraphy and *Hangeul* script, the Korean writing system); "Landscapes of Korea" on the Korean peninsula's natural history and its built landscape; and "Korea Beyond Borders" about the identity of millions of Koreans and their descendants living outside of Korea. In addition, an area of contemporary Korean art illustrates another important theme of the exhibition—that a dynamic modern Korea finds inspiration in the rich traditions of its past.

The phrase greeting visitors at each entrance to the Gallery (*"Welcome to Korea, where the past is always present, and traditions inspire the future"*) summarizes the exhibition's primary theme. The rich cultural heritage of Korea's past informs and serves to inspire much of the dynamism and innovation found today – even in the "new wave" of today's Korean visual and performing arts, film, literature, videogames and other new media. This theme in turn provided us with an important basis for the selection of objects and topics in the exhibition. Our exhibition team, including an advisory group of colleagues from the National Folk Museum of Korea (Seoul), and many other organizations and people working together, built on this connection between ancient past and dynamic present. As part of the exhibition development process, our colleagues at the Smithsonian's Office of Policy and Analysis organized surveys of random samples of museum visitors, to test their level of awareness about Korea, and the effectiveness of various strategies of presenting Korean culture to the public. It is interesting that the strongest images of Korea on the part of American visitors generally included those of North Korean nuclear issues recently in the news, the Korean War (including images from the popular T.V. show "M*A*S*H") and contemporary manufacturing and exports – with little sense of cultural history. At every turn, our exhibition directly confronts visitors with the deep historicity of Korea's contemporary innovations. The sweep of Korea's history is arrayed along the length of the Gallery through ceramics, whose newest examples relate directly to ancient forms. Contemporary paintings, twenty-first century wedding sets for bride and groom, and contemporary art by Korean Americans all present innovative ways of re-interpreting Korea's past today.

Another important goal of the exhibition, however, was to represent the Smithsonian's own history of collecting. The Smithsonian's history is directly tied to the history of relations between Korea and the United States of America. The anthropology department alone within the Smithsonian's National Museum of Natural History (Washington, D.C.) holds a vast and renowned collection of over 4,000 objects of Korean material culture – from common agricultural tools to courtly robes. (This figure does not count the archival manuscripts or library books, nor include the number of objects in the Natural History Museum's biology or mineral science departments, nor artworks in the Smithsonian art museums.) This anthropology department collection represents more than 120 years of active Smithsonian collecting, study, and preservation. The collection includes donations by private individuals, gifts from foreign governments to U.S. officials, and objects collected by U.S. government employees – prized objects directly related to relations between these countries.

Especially noteworthy are the historically unique ethnographic collections brought to the United States in the late nineteenth century by the first American diplomats and missionaries to Korea, including the Bernadou, Jouy, Allen, and Shufeldt collections – all the subject of ongoing research and study.

The exhibition opened in 2007, the 125th anniversary year of the signing of the Treaty of Amity and Commerce between the United States and Korea – Korea's first modern treaty with a foreign government. In the years prior to and following that 1882 treaty, the Smithsonian played an important role as repository for America's national collections assembled by early diplomats and missionaries. Some of these early diplomatic collections are included in the exhibition, and are also the subject of research and publication "behind the scenes" as part of a wider Korean Heritage project, based in the Smithsonian's Asian Cultural History Program.

In addition to Smithsonian objects, the Korea Gallery displays important works loaned from other collections around the world.

## Korea: Exhibitions Viewed from an Integrated Curatorial Program

The Asian Cultural History Program ("ACHP") is just one of many examples of an *integrated curatorial program*, which can be defined as a unit within a museum, responsible for the curation of a specific collection, which also takes on and develops external funding for the full range of museum activities that make collection curation most effective. These minimally should include exhibition, education, outreach, research and publication, and the development and care of museum collections. In many cases, such programs (including the Asian Cultural History Program) also make a substantial contribution to other museum needs.

The development of integrated curatorial programs such as the Asian Cultural History Program has provided a means of finding such synergies, in order to increase productivity and effectiveness as well as public support. By definition, such programs require a curatorial (collection-based) component. The ACHP has been a trust-funded program within the Anthropology Department since 1985. Much of the program's funding, and many of its activities, have since that time been centered on a number of selected "Heritage" projects, each having an integrated approach to exhibition, education, outreach, research, and collection improvement. In 1985, these consisted only of an active "Heritage of Thailand" project – with many associated visiting researchers and with a history of publications, exhibitions, and events – and the "Korean Heritage" project which began that year based on the successful Thai model. As we initiated this second "Heritage" project in 1985, expanding upon the lone example of a dedicated fund and set of activities within our museum about Thailand, we recognized that these examples needed to be placed within a framework of parallel kinds of activities and funding documents. Consequently a new "gift fund" for Korea was established, within a "Program" of the

Jean Baptiste Bernadou (1858-1908) assembled an important Korean
ethnographic collection in 1884 and 1885, one of three early
collections by American diplomats in Korea that were described in
an 1892 monograph by Smithsonian curator Walter Hough.

National Anthropological Archives, Smithsonian Institution

anthropology department, named the "Asian Cultural History Program."

Such a program of activities and goals is enhanced by the selection of a very publicly shared goal which serves as the "flagship of a fleet" of related activities. For the Korean Heritage Project, the Korea Gallery has served as the flagship for many activities. ACHP staff, and especially our many welcome visitors and associates, can become involved in hosting individual events, lectures, films, traveling exhibits, or other activities, at the Natural History Museum and at many other venues.

One key to the success of these Heritage Projects, which applies also to the Korea Gallery, has been the continued maintenance of public involvement. This mode of preparing an exhibition within a larger framework of community involvement reflects a changing view of the nature of museum curatorship as a social practice. Such a view places museum exhibitions within a more holistic, integrated, and culturally relative approach to curatorial work that explores and includes the relationships among (museum) objects, people, and society in social and cultural contexts beyond the museum collection or exhibition. Museum-based projects that include exhibitions increasingly involve integrating events that bring together a community

or communities to celebrate or re-assert shared values, in addition to the traditional curatorial responsibilities, such as the responsibility to preserve and care for collections, to add new information through research on collections, and to accurately interpret and present objects in exhibitions and other media. This involvement of a large community helped to turn a Museum space into a public, multi-generational gathering space for a broad and diverse community of Koreans, Korean-Americans, and many others interested in Korean heritage.

## Early years of Korea and the Smithsonian

As mentioned above, one of the exhibition's goals has been to introduce the Smithsonian's own collections, especially those tied to the early years of U.S.-Korean diplomatic relations. The Smithsonian had an important role as a repository for Korean collections obtained during the earliest period of diplomatic contacts between the Kingdom of Korea and the United States of America. In fact, the Smithsonian's three major Korean ethnographic collections of this period are all by Americans associated with the U.S. diplomatic mission to the Kingdom: John B. Bernadou (1858-1908), whose collection is the first, and the most comprehensive; Horace Newton Allen (1858-1932), a Presbyterian medical missionary who also served as medical officer both to the American Legation (diplomatic mission) and later to the court of Korea's King Kojong; and Pierre Louis Jouy (1856-1894), who assisted with the mission that led to the 1882 treaty and who later became an advisor to the Korean civil service. The collections assembled by these three early diplomats later formed the basis of a report by Smithsonian curator Walter Hough, *The Bernadou, Allen, and Jouy Korean Collections in the United States National Museum* (published in 1892, within the Annual Report of the U.S. National Museum for 1891). That report included information about Korean objects donated to the Smithsonian by five other American collectors of the period as well. These historically important collections were also formed by expatriate Americans who lived in Korea in the 1880s. Less well known is the fact that the Smithsonian's study of these collections was made possible through the assistance of a small expatriate Korean community in America, particularly Byeon Su (1861-1891), Seo Gwan-beom (1859-1897) and Seo Jae-pil (1866-1951).

The John Baptiste Bernadou collection of nineteenth-century Korean artifacts is the subject of a recent Asian Cultural History Program publication, *An Ethnography of the Hermit Kingdom: The J. B. Bernadou Korean Collection 1884-1885, by Chang-su Cho Houchins* (Washington, D.C.: Asian Cultural History Program, Smithsonian Institution, 2004). The collection represents a unique attempt by an amateur American ethnographer to record the material culture of the Korean people at a critical moment in Korea's opening to the West. John Baptiste Bernadou assembled this collection from March 1884 to April 1885 as an attaché (or envoy) of the Smithsonian Institution. Since the Smithsonian, as a trust instrumentality of the U.S. government, serves as America's national museum, Bernadou was attached to the American diplomatic mission in Korea. Both Bernadou and the Smithsonian recognized that a new opportunity to record Korean cultural heritage using the methods of nineteenth-century museum science had now opened up along with the "opening" of Korea heralded by the signing in 1882 of the first Treaty of Amity and Commerce between the Kingdom of Korea and the United States of America.

Long known as the "Hermit Kingdom" for its pre-1880s isolation, Korea, or at least many of the Kingdom's elite citizens, wholeheartedly began a new period of openness to the outside world as a result of the exchanges initiated by this accord. Concurrently, Smithsonian scientists of the early 1880s recognized that a major cultural tradition and a previously unstudied geographical region were then becoming accessible to the

kind of systematizing sciences (including ethnology, and taxonomic studies in biology) in which natural history museums of the time excelled. Evolutionary paradigms prevailed at that time in the comparative study of cultures and civilizations; there was also considerable interest in the spread of particular technological and craft traditions through history and around the globe. Such studies required the collection and classification of a wide range of material culture objects as an essential component of any "ethnography" (that is, the description of a particular culture) that would be most useful for building a science of "ethnology" (that is, the comparative study of cultures, for example by comparing ethnographies). Field ethnographer-collectors therefore recognized the importance of systematically collecting material culture from the widest possible range of classes or subgroups, along with documentation of local terms for objects and information about how and by whom they were used. Ethnographic collectors enthusiastically included and documented everyday village crafts within their collections, right alongside aesthetic masterpieces, sacred ritual items, the paraphernalia of kingly rank, graphic arts and written works of literature, or ethnobotanical specimens (like samples of grain or ginseng). Though not formally trained in anthropology, Bernadou collected for the Smithsonian's natural history museum and seems clearly to have understood the principles of collecting that his Smithsonian correspondents always encouraged.

These unique collections from America's earliest diplomatic contacts with Korea, now held by the anthropology department of the National Museum of Natural History, include fine art objects as well as crafts and ethnographic material culture. Their breadth of scope contrasts with a very different type of collecting featured in Smithsonian art museums such as the Freer Gallery of Art and the Arthur M. Sackler Gallery. The tone for such art collections was set by Charles Langley Freer, whose Korean art collections have been described by Thomas Lawton (*Freer: A Legacy in Art*, Washington, D.C.: Freer Gallery of Art, Smithsonian Institution, 1993), to which many important later collections have been added (see also *Asian Art in the Arthur M. Sackler Gallery: The Inaugural Gift*, by Thomas Lawton *et al.*, Washington, D.C.: Arthur M. Sackler Gallery, Smithsonian Institution, 1987).

New York-based *Korea Ensemble* dancers perform at the opening of the exhibition *A Korean American Century* (January 2003)

## Korean Heritage and the Asian Cultural History Program since 1985

Within the National Museum of Natural History, the Korea Gallery, like several smaller exhibitions and many other public programs before it, began as an initiative of the Korean Heritage Project, founded in 1985 within the Museum's Asian Cultural History Program (which is, in turn, within the Department of Anthropology). The Project's purposes and activities are those listed in the founding document of the "Korean Heritage Fund" (a gift fund within the Smithsonian), namely to "support acquisition, conservation/restoration, and exhibition of Korean collections, and to support research on Korea's Heritage and other Korean cultural activities at the Smithsonian Institution." Every year since then, the Asian Cultural History Program has hosted Korean heritage activities, including exhibitions, films, performances, and lectures. In September 2005, having outgrown the Smithsonian's largest auditorium, the twentieth anniversary of this project was celebrated at the Music Center at Strathmore with a special performance of traditional Korean music and dance by the Chung-Ang Korean Traditional Art Group.

In 1986, one of the first events of the newly founded program was a Korean dance performance held in the Natural History Museum's Baird Auditorium by Kim Mae-ja and the Chang Mu Dance Company.

In 1987, a special reception marked the blessing and unveiling of a Sakyamuni Buddha statue, cast iron with gilt from the 11th century, loaned by the National Museum of Korea. This display was part of the Natural History Museum's former "Hall of Asian Peoples." That same year, SamulNori, a group of expert percussionists and dancers, performed a benefit concert of traditional Korean music and dance for the Korean Heritage Project in Baird Auditorium. A temporary exhibition in the museum's rotunda, entitled, "Korean Heritage at the Smithsonian" was put up around the time of the performance.

This modest, temporary exhibition of 1987 highlighted a few of the museum's historic Korean ethnographic objects. A large and enthusiastic group of supporters (many of whom continued their participation over the decades), gathered for the opening event. Korean Embassy staff and corporate leaders came to hear about the potential for the museum's involvement in Korean studies and Korean cultural events. Even at this early stage and in a modest space, an innovative scope for potential future activities of the Korean Heritage Fund was envisioned. The Smithsonian's talismanic folk painting (*minhwa*) of a heavenly rooster, seen standing on one leg in a watchful pose inside the exhibition case, dates from the late 19th century and was used on gates or doors to safeguard the home. Yet just below this folk painting, to the left, are an arrangement of imperial seals (*oksae*). These seals were used by Korean royalty in the late

19th and early 20th centuries. To the right are archeological specimens originally from the Yi Royal House Museum of Art; none ever belonged to the Smithsonian. How did they get here? In fact, these came from an American veteran of the Korean War, who had purchased them in Korea during the War. In our opinion, whoever sold them could not have had legal title. Working with the Embassy of Korea and the Smithsonian's Office of General Counsel, we had arranged for the person who had them to provide to us permission to study and photograph them, along with his quit-claim to title to the government of Korea. This allowed us to return these objects, after the exhibition, to that country's National Museum, from which they had apparently been removed during the difficult days of the Korean War. Many innovative initiatives of this kind took place throughout the history of the Korean Heritage project.

Later exhibitions included "Contemporary Korean

The calligraphy of Kwon Myoung-won (whose artist's name is "Mookjae") is on display in the Korea Gallery. Here, Mr. Kwon writes visitors' names in Hangeul, the Korean script, during the 2007 Asian Pacific American Crafts Festival at the National Museum of Natural History.

Ceramics," which opened in the Smithsonian's Hall of Asian Peoples in 1997. In 2003, we celebrated the centennial of Korean immigration to the United States with a photographic exhibition entitled "A Korean American Century," which opened in Washington (January 22, 2003) then traveled to five other venues including Los Angeles and New York. During that centennial year, under the leadership of the ACHP's Program Manager, Kyle A. Lemargie, the Korean Heritage Project organized and hosted thirteen events at the Natural History Museum, including popular theatrical and music performances, and even the first-ever Smithsonian fashion show, featuring the works of contemporary designer Lee Young Hee, whose designs were inspired by Joseon

A view of one vitrine from the temporary exhibition "Korean Heritage at the Smithsonian" (1987), Rotunda gallery, National Museum of Natural History

dynasty textiles like those in Smithsonian collections.

The Asian Cultural History Program also works closely with the National Museum of Natural History's Asian Pacific American Heritage Committee, which hosts an annual Crafts Festival, a popular event held each May ("Asian Pacific Heritage Month"). In 2007, just before the Korea Gallery opened in June, Korean watercolor painting done by Ms. Bok Kim and hanguel calligraphy by Mookjae Kwon Myoung-won were among the craft demonstrations.

## The Korea Gallery: A Flagship Exhibition

This very partial list of activities leading up to the Korea Gallery will indicate that the Korea Gallery drew on a long history of community involvement and support, as well as smaller exhibitions and numerous public activities. These had allowed us to experiment with and develop new ways of presenting Korean heritage to a broad public. Themes and ideas drawn from prior exhibitions inspired components of the Korea Gallery on topics such as contemporary Korean ceramics, or the Korean American components of the "Korea Beyond Borders" section. Our work with calligraphers during the annual craft events, and the public interest in Korean fashion, led us to realize the potential popularity of a section on "Hangeul" (Korean script), and the inclusion of contemporary wedding costumes inspired by Joseon Dynasty textiles within the exhibition's section on family life. The likely success of those exhibit components was confirmed by audience testing in 2006 and early 2007.

In 2007, many of the events celebrating the opening of the Gallery were held outside the Natural History Museum, this was very productive for developing new partnerships throughout the Washington region. The "Washington Korea Festival 2007" celebrated the opening of the Smithsonian's Korea Gallery but, unlike the 2003 exhibition's events within our Museum, this Festival included activities throughout the Washington region, well beyond the few held at the National Museum of Natural History. Venues included the Kennedy Center, Arlington's Verizon Center, the Freer Gallery, Johns Hopkins University, George Washington University, AFI Silver Theater and Cultural Center, the National Museum of Women in the Arts, and even a highly successful Korean fashion show at the Hyatt Regency Crystal City (Arlington, Virginia). These activities were brought together as a collaborative project from the Smithsonian, The Korea Foundation, KORUS House (the cultural center of the Embassy of the Republic of Korea), and the National Folk Museum of Korea.

In 2007, changes taking place within the Museum of Natural History included abandoning the former "Vision 2000" plan for the future of exhibitions at the museum. That plan had called for a new Asia Hall that would be built around the area where the Korea Gallery is located, and which would have included the Korea Gallery as the first component of that Hall.

This was the long-term plan under which the gallery had been proposed and accepted. Though the Korea Gallery has now opened, prominently located above the Museum's Constitution Avenue entrance, its integration into any future exhibition plan of the Museum will depend on the eventual development and funding of new long-term plans.

In the meantime, the Korea Gallery serves as the flagship exhibition of the Asian Cultural History Program's very active Korean Heritage Project. The exhibition presents millions of visitors with an introduction to Korea's millennia of history and its distinctive culture through ceramics, paintings, textiles, and sculptures, ranging from the 6th century B.C. to the 21st century. Alongside it, collections-based research and field studies, as well as regular events and performances, continue to include Korea's heritage within the Smithsonian Institution's founding mandate for the "increase and diffusion of knowledge."

***Carving of tiger with two human figures***
Antler, green dye, 7 cm
Undated (collected in 1890s)
Collected by Commodore Robert Shufeldt
Smithsonian, Dept. of Anthropology, E211173

Tigers are an important figure in Korean mythology and folklore.
They appear in stories and art work throughout Korean history.
Spotlighted behind glass in the gallery is a small antler carving,
dyed in dark green, depicting a tiger and two human figures.
This particular piece was collected by U.S. Commodore Robert
Shufeldt in the 1890s. It was Shufeldt who negotiated the first
Treaty of Amity and Commerce between the Kingdom of Korea
and the United States of America in 1892.

# LANDSCAPES OF KOREA

*For thousands of years, Korea's soaring mountains, scenic coasts, and deep forests have inspired the Korean people.*

Many visitors often ask why an exhibit about Korea, which highlights many great pieces of art, is located in a natural history museum and not an art museum. The context of this exhibit, however, is the anthropology and story of the Korean people; a story which is shaped by the natural environment of the Korean peninsula. Visitors can approach this section of the gallery, located directly inside the main exhibit space, from either entrance of the exhibit. It provides an introduction to the physical and cultural environments of Korea, and how the natural landscape influences art and other cultural traditions throughout history and today. Here one can find the oldest artifact in the gallery, a semi-lunar shaped stone knife from the Bronze Age, 6th–5th century B.C.

For thousands of years, Korea's soaring mountains, scenic coasts, and deep forests have inspired the Korean people— including artists and writers, who emphasize harmony between man and nature. Koreans treasure this distinctive landscape, fully conscious of their role in safeguarding the land of their ancestors. A quote printed in the exhibit, from a 16th-century Korean writer, uses the mountain as a symbol of facing challenges:

***Sun, Moon and Five Peaks***
Reproduction courtesy National Palace Museum of Korea

The Sun, Moon, and Five Peaks screen traditionally hung behind the royal palace throne during the Joseon Period (1392 to 1910). Paintings such as these are rich in symbolism, and can be seen in preserved historical palaces in Seoul today. The bold, primary colors in this painting (blue, red, yellow, white, and black) formed the Korean palette and related to the five elements (wood, fire, earth, metal, and water) and five directions (east, south, center, west, and north).

*Semi-lunar knife*
Stone, 15.2 x 6.4 cm
6th–5th century B.C., Bronze age
Collected by P. L. Jouy
Smithsonian, Dept. of Anthropology,
A140905

This knife was probably used by ancestors of present-day
Koreans to harvest rice, a staple of the Korean diet.

**Korean ginseng (root)**
*Panax schinseng Nees*
49.5 x 19 cm
Loaned by Kim's Acupuncture

Called the "elixir of life" and "king of the herbs," Korean ginseng is nearly extinct in its native mountainous habitat. But the plant has been cultivated for centuries, and it is now raised on large farms and exported around the world as a health supplement.

*"The mountain may be high
But it is still below heaven.
Climb and climb again;
Everyone can reach the summit.
Only the man who never tried
Insists the mountain is high."*
—Yang Sa-eon, (1517–1584)

A satellite image on one side of the gallery shows the mountainous landscape of the Korean peninsula. Mountains cover about 70 percent of the peninsula, forming a spine along the east coast. The west coast has many scenic bays and inlets. Although Korea has no active volcanoes, it does experience minor earthquakes. On the opposite side of the gallery is another satellite image, taken at night, which illustrates Korea's built landscape and the difference between South Korea, which is covered in lights, and North Korea, which is primarily dark. Featured photographs depict the mountains and sea coasts of the peninsula, the weather representing all four seasons, and the skyline of modern cities. A banner hanging above the gallery also provides a visual backdrop which displays many scenes of nature. With a climate much like the northern United States, Korea is home to some 400 species of animals and 3,000 species of plants. Until the late 19th century, Korea was largely agricultural with farms carved out of the hilly landscape. Archeological evidence shows that humans lived here 500,000 years ago. It is not known what happened to these early residents, but present-day Koreans descend from people who migrated during the past 30,000 years from what is now southern Siberia, China, and Mongolia.

Detail: *Carving of tiger with two human figures* (see p. 34).

*Bowl*
Stoneware, celadon glaze,
7 x 19.5 cm
12th century, Goryeo
Smithsonian, Dept. of
Anthropology, E167587
Restored in 2006,
Korea Gallery Fund

# A History in Ceramics

*For thousands of years, Korean potters produced high-quality ceramics from delicate celadons to functional storage jars.*

*Many of these ancient forms continue to inspire contemporary ceramists in Korea and around the world.*

One of the main features of the Korea Gallery is a historical "timeline" of ceramics, running across the length of the exhibit and positioned in front of traditional Korean latticework. Here visitors can see, through original ceramic pieces, how artistic styles evolved over the years according to advancements in technology and other needs. For thousands of years, Korean potters produced high-quality ceramics from delicate celadons to functional storage jars. Although influenced by Chinese traditions, Koreans developed their own techniques, shapes, and decorative styles. Many of these ancient forms continue to inspire contemporary ceramists in Korea and around the world.

The Korea Gallery exhibit space is unique because a significant amount of natural light floods into the hallway from several large windows. While this provides a bright and comfortable setting which is different from the traditionally dark exhibit hall, it also prohibits the use of certain fragile materials such as paper that could easily be damaged over time. Fortunately, ceramics are sturdy enough to be displayed in this setting. Further, they provide an excellent visual aid with which to tell the history of Korea. Visitors can begin on the far left of the exhibit (facing the windows) and walk their way from the earliest kingdoms

**Incised bowl (3 views)**
Stoneware, celadon, 7 x 23 cm
Late 20th century
By Kwang-yeol Yoo
Smithsonian, Dept. of Anthropology,
E431761

E431762

*Onggi*
Stoneware, 12 x 14.5 cm
19th century
Collected by J. B. Bernadou
Smithsonian, Dept. of
Anthropology, E121617

*Onggi* jars have been a fixture of every Korean household for centuries.
Traditionally, *onggi* (pronounced OHNG-ghee) stored different sauces, grains, and foods
such as kimchi, a Korean dish of fermented vegetables and spices. The *onggi*, which means
stoneware jar, has changed very little over the past several centuries.

*Onggi*
Stoneware, 35.5 x 32.5 cm
20th century
Loaned by KI Graphics, Inc.

period to the modern period or, start from the modern era and browse backwards in time. Each period includes a brief synopsis of the historical events, and political and cultural themes that prevailed during the era. This background information is presented in "flip-books," positioned between the ceramic cases. Also on display are three celadon tiles, representing different stages in the firing process, which visitors are encouraged to touch to examine how such ceramics with inlaid designs are crafted.

Celadons represent one of Korea's most significant cultural legacies. Two bowls, one from the 12th century (pictured on page 42) and another from the late 20th century (pages 44-45), are separated by 800 years, and demonstrate Korea's continued interest in the classic celadon glaze, sometimes described as having the radiance of jade and clarity of water.

The ceramic pieces selected for display in the Korea Gallery are drawn mostly from the Smithsonian's collection, supplemented by important examples from private collectors.

**Pot and stand**
Stoneware, 54 x 23 cm
5th–6th century, Silla
Collected by P. L. Jouy
Smithsonian, Dept. of Anthropology, A552439 (pot), A552492 (stand)

Excavated from a Silla tomb, this pot probably held a food offering.
Stands like this might have been used during outdoor public rituals.

# Earliest Kingdoms (57 B.C. – 935A.D.)

*Silla royal tombs were decorated with elaborate wall paintings and filled with jewelry, arms and armor, pottery, food offerings, and spectacular gold crowns.*

Tribal federations evolved into independent, centralized states ruled by kings during this time. By the sixth century, three large kingdoms—Goguryeo, Baekje, and Silla—and a small federation called Gaya competed for trade and alliance with China. In 668, the Silla (pronounced SHIL-la) defeated the other kingdoms, ending centuries of conflict. Buddhism slowly spread from China and each kingdom adopted it as a state religion, which later helped build support for national unity.

Ancient tombs preserve many objects that reveal Korea's distant past. In Gyeongju, capital of Unified Silla, hill-shaped tombs have yielded many clues about this period of Korean history. They are now protected as a national park. Silla royal tombs were decorated with elaborate wall paintings and filled with jewelry, arms and armor, pottery, food offerings, and spectacular gold crowns. Such items honored the deceased and equipped them for the afterlife. Pierre Louis Jouy, a Smithsonian scientist during the late 19th century, assembled a collection of 64 early Korean mortuary ceramics, several of which are on display in the gallery.

Korean potters constructed hill-climbing kilns with sloping floors to take advantage

**Animal-shaped pendant**
Stone, 6.9 x 10.3 cm
probably 5th–6th century
Collected by P. L. Jouy
Smithsonian, Dept. of Anthropology,
A140910

Collected for the Smithsonian in 1888, this object was said to have come from a hill-shaped tomb in southern Korea. The hole suggests that it may have been a pendant, possibly hung from a belt. Some Korean scholars believe it represents a dragon, but like many ancient objects, its purpose and symbolism is debatable.

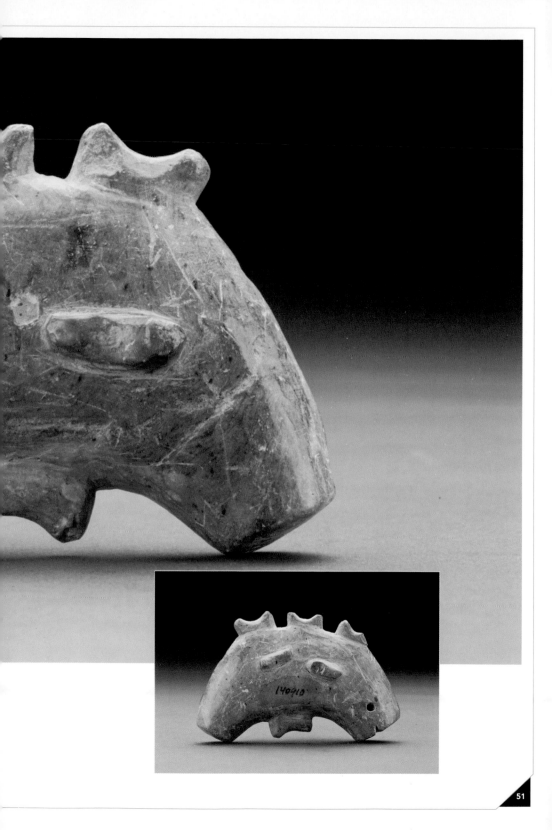

*Oil lamp*
Stoneware, 16.5 x 22 cm
5th–6th century, Silla
Collected by P. L. Jouy
Smithsonian, Dept. of Anthropology,
A552493

Wheel-thrown cups were joined on
a ring and foot. The hollow ring
enabled oil to flow evenly among the
cups, which contained wicks.

of the physics of rising heat. The fire was built inside the bottom opening, and the flames and heat swept up over the pots and out the top. To make a durable ceramic, the kiln needed to produce high temperatures. During the Joseon period, potters built their kilns on hillsides to generate greater heat for firing porcelain. The potter's wheel, a small, rapidly spinning turntable for shaping clay, came to Korea from China between the first and third centuries. As its use spread, production increased. When Koreans began making large storage pots known as onggi centuries later, they used a wheel set into the ground as a turntable on which to coil the large, heavy forms. The Three Kingdoms and Unified Silla periods produced some of the earliest stoneware in the world, a ceramic made from a type of clay that can be fired at high temperatures to become hard like stone.

**Bowl with impressed cicada design**
Stoneware, 9 x 17 cm
8th century, Unified Silla
Smithsonian, Dept. of Anthropology,
A455472

The cicada design may symbolize the transformation from life to afterlife. After a cicada emerges from the ground, the insect sheds its skin or nymph shell.

***Lidded bowl with impressed design***
Stoneware, 15 x 20 cm
8th–9th century, Unified Silla
Anonymous donor
Smithsonian, Dept. of Anthropology, A450063

The potter stamped designs into the wet clay just after throwing it on the potter's wheel. The lid, when inverted, doubles as a dish. The slight sheen on the surface is a natural glaze that formed when ash fell on the bowl during firing.

*Mirror*
Bronze, 16.5 cm
Goryeo
Loaned by Dr. Chester and Mrs. Wanda Chang

Bronze mirrors were essential accessories for women of the Goryeo court. The mirrors were also placed in tombs to quiet spirits. *Translation of Chinese* (seal script): bright and great shining heaven.

# Goryeo Dynasty (918 – 1392 A.D.)

During the Goryeo (pronounced KO-ree-o) dynasty, the government grew more centralized and extended its control to regulating differences between the ruling and lower classes. Buddhism enjoyed lavish patronage and became so integrated into the state that no king ruled without first becoming a monk. Under state patronage, wooden printing blocks of the complete Buddhist sacred texts (called the *Tripitaka Koreana*) were carved as an act of faith to gain protection of the Buddha in the 11th century. These were destroyed during the Mongol invasion of 1231-1232. A second set of 81,137 blocks was completed in 1251 and today is stored at Haeinsa Temple (South Korea).

*The Goryeo court financed many scholarly pursuits and inventions, including development of cast-metal movable type nearly two centuries before Gutenberg in Europe.*

The Goryeo court financed many scholarly pursuits and inventions, including development of cast-metal movable type nearly two centuries before Gutenberg in Europe. During its later years, the dynasty was periodically ravaged by invaders, including Mongols in the 13th century. Mongols invaded Korea six times between 1231 and 1252. During the 100 years that the Mongols ruled Goryeo, its kings took Mongol names and spoke the Mongol language, and Korean princes married Mongol princesses. A number of Mongol traditions were adopted including long hair ribbons (seen in the wedding dress on display in the exhibit) and other clothing. Koreans also borrowed many Mongol hunting traditions such as the tunic style and the use of horses.

China greatly influenced Goryeo politics and culture. Koreans adopted Chinese conventions such as a central bureaucracy, civil service examinations, and government factories that produced goods for the court during this period.

Celadon is the most famous and highly valued of Korean pottery. The glaze and firing technique originated in China, but by the 12th century, Goryeo potters had invented new techniques and forms. Chinese collectors of this period declared Korean celadon one of the "wonderful products" of the world. Celadon refers to a glaze color that emulates jade ranging from green to blue-gray. Koreans call celadon bi-saek, or secret color.

One of the interesting (non-ceramic) pieces in this section of the gallery is a bronze mirror (pictured on the cover and p. 56). While these mirrors were found in tombs in Korea, they are also found in China during this same time period of the Song dynasty (960-1279 AD). It remains unclear if these mirrors were originally made in China and ended up being placed in Korean burial sites, or if Korean artists adopted or reinterpreted the design of the Chinese mirrors. Both the Chinese and Koreans shared the belief that the mirrors served an important function in the after-life or spirit world. In the scene depicted on the mirror, a sail boat and its passengers are confronted with a dragon in a cloud. Scholars have theorized that the dragon might be a protective guide for the eight souls in the boat as they travel into the next life and that perhaps these passengers represent the "Eight Immortals" of Taoist folklore. It has also been suggested that the scene might illustrate the story of the Korean monk Uisang (625-702) and the legend of the girl who fell in love with him and transformed into a dragon to protect and follow him on his voyage at sea.

*Fluted bottle*
Stoneware, celadon glaze, 22.5 x 14 cm
10th–11th century, Goryeo
Smithsonian, Dept. of Anthropology, E401646

The shape and glaze on this bottle are modeled after Yue wares, the official ware of the Wu-Yue court of 10th-century China.

***Bowl***
Stoneware, celadon glaze, 5.5 x 14 cm
10th–11th century, Goryeo
Smithsonian, Dept. of Anthropology, E121618

This bowl is closely related to Chinese Yue celadon ware. It was probably
used for drinking tea. The color of celadon was considered a good aesthetic
complement to tea.

**Maebyeong bottle**
Stoneware, celadon glaze, 30.2 x 18.5 cm
12th century, Goryeo
Loan from Freer Study Collection, FSC-P-3890

The shape of this bottle—the tall profile, broad shoulder, and small
opening—is based on the Chinese meiping, meaning plum bottle.

***Water vessel (kundika)***
Stoneware, celadon glaze, 32 x 11 x 15 cm
12th century, Goryeo
Smithsonian, Dept. of Anthropology, E121612

During the 12th century, kundika were used by all classes of Koreans for storing water.
Water was poured from the top spout and refilled from the side spout. It was traditionally
used to sprinkle water in Buddhist rituals. Clay spurs on this vessel's foot and the color
of the glaze show that it was made at a provincial kiln. If it had been made at a central
government kiln, silica chips would have been used.

**Bottle**
Stoneware, 33 x 18 cm
11th–13th century, Goryeo
Smithsonian, Dept. of Anthropology, A407251

The unglazed stoneware tradition continued during the Goryeo period as an affordable alternative to celadon. The hole in the bottle's narrow neck admitted air to make pouring easier.

***Bottle with chrysanthemum pattern***
Stoneware, inlaid celadon glaze, 31.5 x 16 cm
13th century, Goryeo
Smithsonian, Dept. of Anthropology, E402856

In the 12th century, Goryeo potters invented and mastered the inlay process, an
extremely complicated technique. Each flower petal was delicately carved into the
clay and then filled with a mixture of clay and quartz that fired white. Different mixes
turned black, dark red, or brown when fired.

### Flask with flower design
Stoneware, *buncheong* ware, 21 x 19 x 12 cm
15th–16th century, Joseon
Smithsonian, Dept. of Anthropology, E409150

The freely drawn flower carved through the clay slip achieves the
distinctive *buncheong* style. A wheel-thrown jar was flattened into
this shape, commonly used to hold liquor.

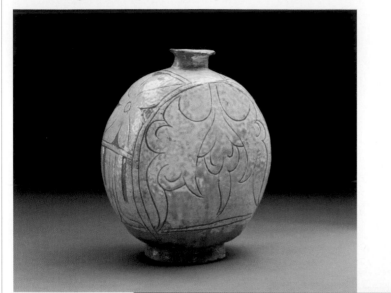

### Bowl with inlaid designs
Stoneware, *buncheong* ware, 8 x 19.5 cm
15th–16th century, Joseon
Smithsonian, Dept. of Anthropology,
E401653

This bowl's decoration is a simplification of the inlay technique
typical of Goryeo celadons, using stamped designs and white slip.

# Joseon Dynasty (1392 – 1910 A.D.)

The Joseon dynasty was one of the longest in world history. Joseon (pronounced CHO-sun) rulers established a social hierarchy based on Confucian principles that emphasized key interpersonal relationships—ruler to citizen, father to son, husband to wife, elder brother to younger brother, and friend to friend. Joseon is based on two borrowed Chinese roots meaning morning and fresh. Even today, Korea is known as The Land of Morning Calm.

The ruling elite were the yangban (pronounced YAHNG-bahn) class of Confucian scholars. A middle class consisted of minor officials and professionals like doctors, and a commoner class included farmers and craftsmen such as potters. Slaves and those with undesirable occupations such as shamans and butchers made up the lowest class.

A male member of the aristocratic yangban class was expected to be a model of Confucian propriety and learning—a student of the Chinese classics and someone who acted courteously and righteously.

*"...he [a yangban] must read aloud the classics, line after line, as quickly and as smoothly as a gourd dipper rolls across the*

*Joseon is based on two borrowed Chinese roots meaning morning and fresh. Even today, Korea is known as The Land of Morning Calm.*

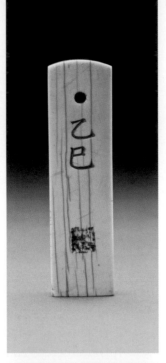

*Ivory tag*
10.8 x 2.8 cm
Translation from Chinese:
Hong Gi-seop; born 1842;
passed civil service exam
in 1864. ◄

*Wood tag*
9.2 x 2.2 cm
Translation from Chinese:
Yuhak Gim Muk-gon, also
known as Nakyu; student;
not yet passed exam, born
in Janghuing Pyeongho
in 1857. ►

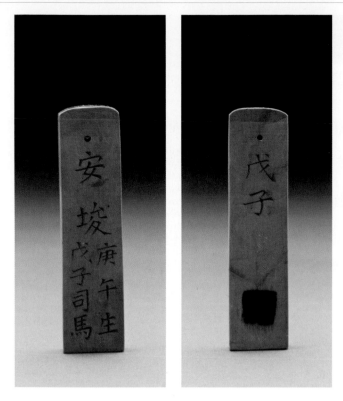

**Wood tag**
8.9 x 2.2 cm
Translation from Chinese:
An Jun; born 1870; earned
the rank of chief of the office
dealing with arms and war
horses in 1888. ◄

**Identity tags (Hopae)**
Ivory, wood, late 19th & early 20th century
Collected by C. Paul Dredge and Yigu Kwon; gifts of Virgil Hillyer Fund
Smithsonian, Dept. of Anthropology, E418342, E418341, E415031

In Joseon's ordered social structure, males 15 years or older wore tags
with their name, birthplace, birth date, and level passed on government
tests. The government used the tags to keep official records. An ivory
tag indicated high rank.

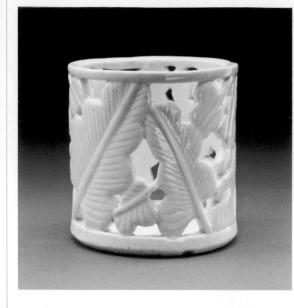

**Brush holder**
Porcelain, 12.5 x 12 cm
19th century, Joseon
Donated by Gustavus Goward
Smithsonian, Dept. of
Anthropology, E209173

A brush holder was an essential
part of every scholar's study, as
was the brush, ink stone, ink
stick, and paper. Joseon scholars
were expected to be accomplished
at calligraphy. Only members of
the aristocratic *yangban* class had
the time and education to pursue
a scholarly life.

ice. He must walk in a dignified
manner, stepping lightly with
his feet turned outward...."
—The Tale of a Yangban
by Pak Chiwon (1737–1805)
translated by Giles Ryan

As Confucianism grew in
Korea during the 17th century,
the role of yangban women
changed. They were generally
expected to remain silent and
obedient in public and were
not allowed to hold property.
They spent most days at home
because strict social codes
separated men and women.
When women went outside,
they wore a coat-shaped
garment over their heads,
revealing only their eyes and
nose, to shield themselves from
any men they might meet.

Buncheong (pronounced
POON-chong) stoneware used
iron-bearing clay decorated with
designs drawn or inlaid with
white slip (a thick solution of
white clay and water). Because
the process for buncheong
evolved from celadon, many
of its shapes and decorative
patterns are similar. Yet
buncheong also shows simpler,
freer, and more abstract designs.
All classes used these ceramics.
Production of buncheong ceased
when many kilns were destroyed
during the Japanese invasions of
1592 and 1598.

***Bottle with dragon design***
Porcelain with cobalt decoration, 30 x 16 cm
Late 19th century, Joseon
Collected by J. B. Bernadou
Smithsonian, Dept. of Anthropology, E401648

A product of the government workshops, this bottle probably served wine. The dragon is a classic symbol of benevolent male power. It was probably drawn by a professional painter, using cobalt pigment, and covered with a clear, slightly bluish glaze.

**Jar with auspicious symbols**
Porcelain with cobalt decoration,
14.6 x 15.2 cm
18th–19th century, Joseon
Loaned by Dr. Chester and
Mrs. Wanda Chang

Typically found in women's quarters,
jars like this vessel stored cooking
sauces. The decorations are symbols
of wealth and prosperity, including
cash, peony, and tied scrolls.

White porcelain wares were
made with kaolin (white
porcelain clay), fired at a high
temperature, and covered
with a transparent glaze.
The all-white ceramics were
valued for their understated
elegance which mirrored
Confucian ideals of restraint
and simplicity. White wares
were originally produced for
government and provincial
offices, but by the 18th century,
they were also found in upper
class homes. Joseon kilns also

*Incense burner*
Porcelain with cobalt decoration, 14 x 25 cm
19th century, Joseon
Donated by H. B. Hulbert
Smithsonian, Dept. of Anthropology,
E167685

This shape, made with a mold, features a plum blossom motif, an emblem of the royal court and symbol of courage and nobility. Typically, the container would have held lit incense sticks set into ash.

produced porcelain decorated with blue, brown, or red pigments.

Although potters belonged to Korea's lower class, their work was highly valued. During the Japanese invasions of 1592 and 1598, many Korean potters were forcibly taken to Japan. They made significant contributions to Japanese ceramics by introducing the hill-climbing kiln and the technology for producing porcelain.

*Jar with abstract design*
Stoneware, inlaid celadon, 35 cm
1998
By Bang Chul-ju (artist name Hyuck San)
Loaned by the artist

This jar simultaneously reflects the influence of the inlaid celadon tradition, invented by Korean potters nearly 900 years ago, and a modern aesthetic influenced by international art movements.

# Modern Period (1910 – Present)

*One of the key factors in South Korea's success was its shipbuilding industry, which built many of the ships and containers that helped produce the economic boom of the 20th century.*

The last 100 years brought tremendous change to the land once called by outsiders the Hermit Kingdom. As Korea came into contact with the West and other nations at the end of the 19th century, the Korean people faced many challenges—including the Japanese occupation (1910–1945). The country, unified for more than a millennium, was divided into two countries at the end of World War II, a Soviet-allied North and a U.S.-allied South. Tensions between the two countries resulted in the Korean War (1950–1953). When the conflict was over more than 1,500,000 people were wounded or killed. Many families were separated by the division of Korea and could not contact each other for decades. By the early 21st century, both North and South Korea had an important presence on the world stage. Despite their shared heritage, the South's industrial and economic growth and its openness to travel and commerce have accentuated the differences between the two nations.

In 1960, South Korea was economically one of the least developed countries in the world. In only 20 years, through a mixture of market-friendly and state-controlled economic policies known as planned capitalism, the nation transformed itself into an economic powerhouse. One of the key factors in South Korea's success was

*Tea/coffee cup and saucer*
Stoneware, 7.6 x 12.7 cm
2006
Donated by Icheon Ceramics
Company (Korea)

Like many 20th-century arts, mass production of ceramics in large workshops made quality works more accessible to Koreans. The classic Korean *buncheong* style was adapted to this western-style cup and saucer.

its shipbuilding industry, which built many of the ships and containers that helped produce the economic boom of the 20th century. By the beginning of the 21st century, South Korea had become one of the world's largest economies.

During the last half-century, North Korea remained a Communist state, even as financial support from China and Russia declined. Premier Kim Il Sung (r. 1945–1994) and his son Kim Jong Il (r. 1994 to present) have ruled the country with unchallenged power. A radically reshaped Korean society practices very simplified versions of ancient Korean ancestor traditions.

Some celebrations, like the 60th birthday, have been abolished.

During the 20th century, Korean potters began signing their ceramics in response to an international fine art market that values the work of individual artists. Contemporary artists strive to distinguish their works through experimentation and individual expression. But the artistic vocabulary of many Korean potters still relies on classic shapes and styles from the Goryeo and Joseon periods.

**Bottle**
Stoneware, *buncheong* ware, 33 x 32 cm
Late 20th century
By Yik-yung Kim
Smithsonian, Dept. of Anthropology,
E431741

Although the shape and technique of
this bottle recall the wine flask in the
Joseon section, the large size and the
design on just one side mark it as an
art object meant for display rather than
practical use.

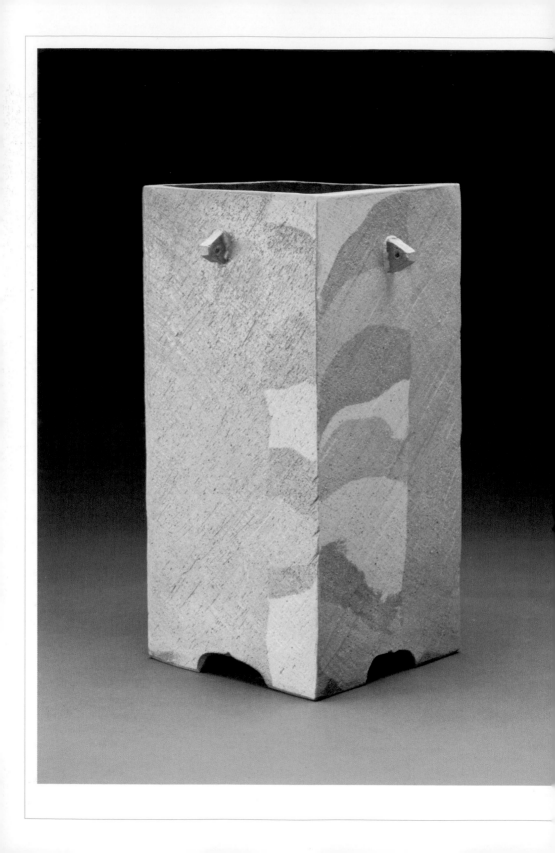

***Marbleized ceramic vase***
Stoneware, 32.7 x 15.7 cm
Late 20th century
By Kyung-joe Roe
Smithsonian, Dept. of Anthropology, E431753

Many Korean art potters today work in an international style that is beyond cultural boundaries. This vase was hand-built, making artistic use of different types of clay that fire in different colors.

***Woodblock of hangeul syllabary***
Wood, 45 x 19.5 cm
19th century
Collected by J. B. Bernadou
Smithsonian, Dept. of Anthropology, ECC77018

Sheets of paper printed from this woodblock were used to teach the *hangeul* syllables and other subjects. In the center of the woodblock is a table that shows the properly formed syllables. The small animals along the top edge helped teach the sounds of letters. The *hangeul* syllables read from top to bottom.

# Hangeul

Standing directly inside one entrance of the Korea Gallery is a display case dedicated to hangeul (pronounced HAHN-guhl), the alphabet of the Korean language. The invention of this writing system in the 15th century is a significant achievement in the history of Korean scholarship. With the help of commissioned scholars, King Sejong, whose image appears in this display, created a script based on the sounds of the spoken language. Hangeul was used for informal genres like household manuals, Buddhist texts, and light fiction. But for centuries after its invention, formal documents and scholarly works used Chinese characters to write Korean words. The first hangeul newspapers appeared in the late 1800s. Hangeul was forbidden as being nationalistic during the Japanese colonial period (1910–1945). After the Korean War (1953), hangeul was adopted as the official written language. A great source of national pride, hangeul is also studied by Koreans living outside of Korea.

*With the help of commissioned scholars, King Sejong created a script based on the sounds of the spoken language.*

Korean calligraphy is modeled after the Chinese scholarly tradition which combines artistic expression with a well-balanced and skillful composition. Until recently, most Korean calligraphy used Chinese rather than hangeul. The items on display in the Korea Gallery represent typical

***Hangeul calligraphy (Yongbi eocheonga)***
Paper, ink, 140 x 82 cm
2006
By Mookjae Kwon Myoung-won

Translation of calligraphy:
*Trees with deep roots do not sway in the wind,*
*But bear fine flowers and bountiful fruit,*
*Water welling from deep springs never dries up,*
*But becomes rivers and flows to the seas.*
—from *Songs of Flying Dragons*, the first work to be written in
*hangeul* and commissioned by King Sejong.

objects that would be used by a calligrapher. There is also an interactive display that teaches visitors how some simple words are formed using hanguel.

Today there are 24 basic letters in the Korean writing system: 14 consonants and 10 vowels. Like English writing, hangeul is based on phonetics. Once you learn the sounds of the letters, you can sound out many words. To write a Korean word in hangeul, you group the letters that sound out a syllable into a block. Usually a syllable has about two to three letters, but it can include more. These syllable blocks are further grouped into words.

For example:

한 국

[3 hangeul letters] • [3 hangeul letters]
H    a    n    •    g eu l

*Hangeul* means script of the Han people.

**Brushes (But)**
Examples of brushes used for calligraphy
Brush (left), 28 cm
Brush (center), 31 cm
Brush (right), 27 cm

**Brush holder (Piltong)**
Porcelain, 12.5 x 10 cm
20th century
Donated by National Museum of Korea
Smithsonian, Dept. of Anthropology,
E424683

*Ink stone (Byeoru)*
Stone, 23.5 x 15 x 3.8 cm
Undated
Gift of Virgil Hillyer Fund
Smithsonian, Dept. of Anthropology, E418371

**_Water dropper (Yeonjeok)_**
Porcelain with cobalt decoration, 7 cm
19th–20th century
Gift of Virgil Hillyer Fund
Smithsonian, Dept. of Anthropology, E418375

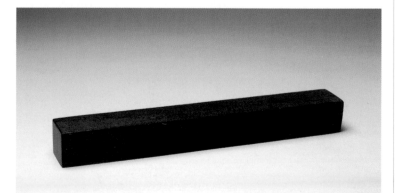

**_Paperweight (Munjin)_**
Stone, undated, 21.8 x 2.5 x 3 cm
Gift of Virgil Hillyer Fund
Smithsonian, Dept. of Anthropology, E418361

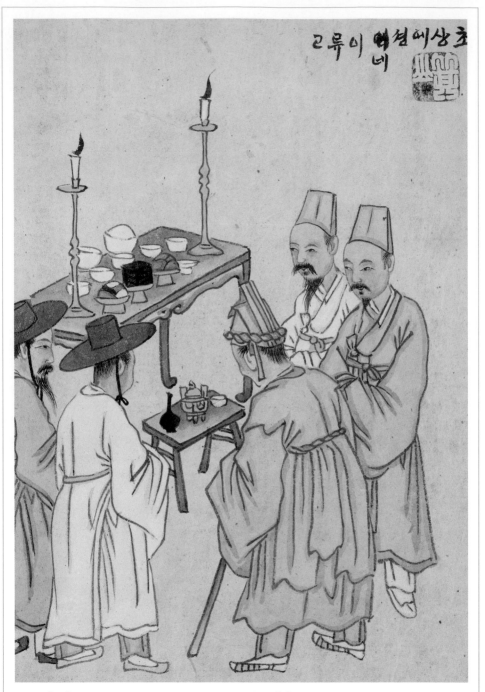

*Chief Mourner Receives Visitors Paying Condolences, 1886.*
This 19th-century print shows how Korean mourners typically received
visitors and presented food offerings.
National Anthropological Archives, Smithsonian Institution,
INV08571400

# THE KOREAN FAMILY

Some of the rich cultural traditions of the Korean family are illustrated in the Korea Gallery. The importance of honoring family and ancestors, celebrating marriage, and birthdays, are all featured here.

Paying respect to one's elders, both living and dead, has deep roots in Korea, originating in Confucian principles which emphasize serving one's parents and ancestors. Koreans honor their deceased relatives with offerings at an ancestral altar. To the family, the spirits of the dead are always present and can act as guardians or benefactors. The practice of placing offerings at altars to honor ancestors was initially banned by some Christian leaders, but now the practice has been re-interpreted as simply showing respect for one's elders. A reproduction of a Korean military official portrait from the early 18th century stands beside the ancestor altar in the exhibit. To the Korean family, the formal portrait served as a symbol of prestige and record of nobility. Portraits would be hung in the home to honor the family's ancestors. To convey the status of this officer, the artist includes a samo, a hat worn by Korean officials; a brocade robe worn by courtiers; and a badge, or hyungbae, with a mythical white tiger, which indicates military rank. The high level of detail and facial expression also

*Paying respect to one's elders, both living and dead, has deep roots in Korea, originating in Confucian principles which emphasize serving one's parents and ancestors.*

***Ancestor Altar***
Wood furniture
20th century
Gift of Yong In University

An ancestor altar like this one can often be found in traditional Korean homes. On the table the family places incense and offerings such as rice wine. Inside the tablet holder they place one or more tablets (sheets of paper or stone), each containing the name of a deceased family member.

Ancestor altar chair *(Gyoui)*, 125 x 47 x 25 cm
Tablet holder *(Wi Pae)*, on top of altar chair, 31 x 17 x 14 cm
Offering table *(Jesasang)*, 84 x 101 x 70 cm
Incense table *(Hyangsang)*, 41.5 x 42.5 x 26.5 cm

***Wedding ducks (Jonan)***
Wood, paint, 33 x 15.2 cm
Late 20th century
Gift of Lee Young Hee Museum

Today, a pair of ducks is usually presented to the couple as a symbol of
fidelity because ducks mate for life. Traditionally the groom gave his
mother-in-law a single carved, wooden duck.

***Wrapping cloth (Bojagi)***
Silk
20th century
Gift of Lee Young Hee Museum
Korean wrapping cloths were an integral part of everyday life among all classes of people during the Joseon dynasty. Today many Koreans wrap wedding gifts with a special quilted cloth *(bojagi)*, thought to capture and hold the intended good wishes.

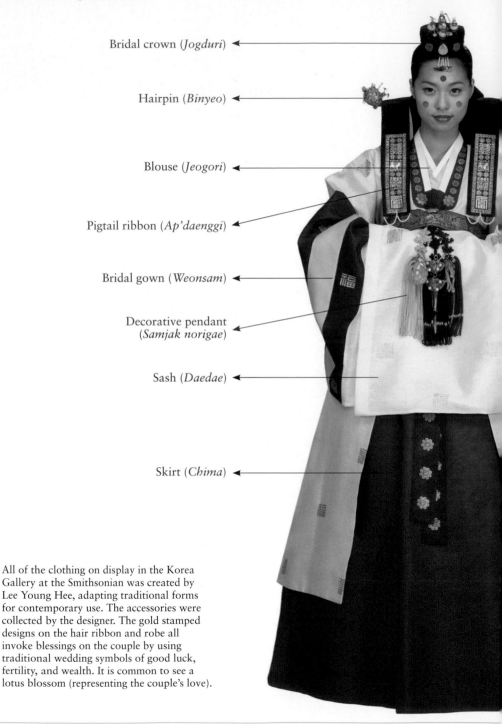

***Bride and groom clothing and accessories***
20th century
Gift of Lee Young Hee Museum

Bridal crown (*Jogduri*)

Hairpin (*Binyeo*)

Blouse (*Jeogori*)

Pigtail ribbon (*Ap'daenggi*)

Bridal gown (*Weonsam*)

Decorative pendant
(*Samjak norigae*)

Sash (*Daedae*)

Skirt (*Chima*)

All of the clothing on display in the Korea
Gallery at the Smithsonian was created by
Lee Young Hee, adapting traditional forms
for contemporary use. The accessories were
collected by the designer. The gold stamped
designs on the hair ribbon and robe all
invoke blessings on the couple by using
traditional wedding symbols of good luck,
fertility, and wealth. It is common to see a
lotus blossom (representing the couple's love).

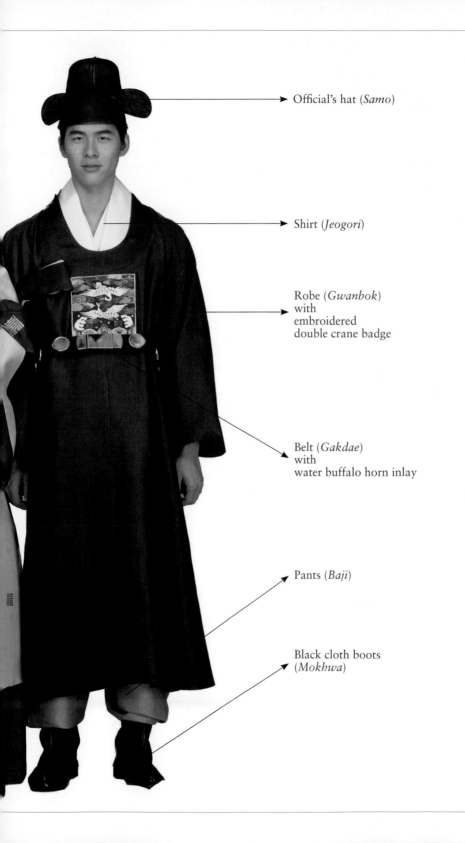

Official's hat (*Samo*)

Shirt (*Jeogori*)

Robe (*Gwanbok*)
with
embroidered
double crane badge

Belt (*Gakdae*)
with
water buffalo horn inlay

Pants (*Baji*)

Black cloth boots
(*Mokhwa*)

**Decorative pendant
(Samjak norigae)**
with jeweled butterfly, coral branch,
jade, and amber.
17.8 x 33 cm

*Bridal crown (Jogduri)*
12.7 x 11.4 cm

*Belt (Gakdae)*
with water buffalo horn inlay
34.3 x 40.6 x 5 cm

*Embroidered shoes
(Kkotsin)*
25.4 x 8.9 cm

demonstrate the importance of the official.

Korean weddings celebrate a courtly past. Many of the beautiful clothes and rituals originated during the Joseon dynasty (1392–1910). At that time only members of the court, shamans, and performers dressed colorfully, and commoners had to wear white. One exception was a wedding, when the bride, groom, and others as well, donned colorful, courtly clothes.

Until the 20th century, weddings were meant to join families of similar status. The bride's role was to continue the ancestral lineage of the husband. Although arranged marriages still exist, a forced union against the individual's wishes is a thing of the past. Contemporary Korean weddings combine Western and Korean traditions. Many couples wear Western dress during the ceremony and change into Korean clothes to greet and bow to their families.

To Koreans, a child's 100th day and first birthday are important celebrations for the family. At first birthday parties, the honored child chooses from an array of auspicious objects which symbolize the child's possible future. This act is considered more of a blessing than a fortunetelling. Sometimes contemporary Korean families include popular objects like a computer mouse and a golf ball. In the exhibit, a small interactive display for children allows them to choose a particular auspicious object and find out what that object symbolizes.

Another especially significant birthday is the 60th. Sixty is important astrologically, because it completes a full cycle according to the Korean zodiac. This custom arose when it was rare for Koreans to reach the age of 60. Now, Koreans live longer, so many families throw big parties to honor their elders' 70th and 80th birthdays.

*Hairpin (Binyeo)*
42 cm

**60th birthday ceremony**
Collection of Chang-su Houchins

In 1932, a Korean family gathered to celebrate the grandfather's 60th birthday. The tall stacks of food and the decorations with Chinese ideographs (meaning congratulations) followed centuries-old traditions.

***Leaving Along the Path Like This***
By Byun Shi-ji
Oil on canvas, 2006, 168 x 118 cm
Loaned by the artist

# CHANGING EXHIBITIONS AND FUTURE INITIATIVES

*The exhibit features (at the time of the opening) a section called "Korea Beyond Borders," and a section on contemporary Korean art, which we hope regularly to change, including new examples and themes.*

The future goals of the Korea gallery include regular enhancements, and especially changes over time to particular portions of the Gallery. The exhibit features (at the time of the opening) a section called "Korea Beyond Borders," and a section on contemporary Korean art, which we hope regularly to change, including new examples and themes. Those enhancements to the Gallery itself constitute just one type of the future initiatives for Korean heritage in the Museum's Asian Cultural History Program, an integrated program of exhibition, collection development, research and publication, education, and community involvement.

## Korea Beyond Borders: Introductions

The section called "Korea Beyond Borders" aims to introduce individual Koreans (or persons of Korean descent), within the larger context of Korean identity beyond the borders of the Republic of Korea. These individuals have stories of broad or universal appeal, but also represent different ways in which Korean identity has been transformed beyond the physical borders of the two political entities of Korea (north or south) as nations. The people of North and South Korea share a cultural identity despite vast differences in political systems and one of the most heavily fortified borders in the world. In addition, millions of Koreans now live outside Korea but still celebrate Korean holidays and traditions in their new countries.

This section of the exhibition introduces Korean immigration to America (using selected photos along with the example of a Korean American artist), as well as Koreans in Central Asia, Koreans who excel in sports at home and abroad, and one of many Koreans whose story reflects the difficult relations between North and South Korea.

## Korean American Artist
Y. David Chung (b. 1959) sees the onggi, a familiar and uniquely Korean houseware, as a container of culture and history. Here, he has fermented or pickled Korea's past by pairing classic Korean auspicious symbols—water, mountain peaks, mushrooms, clouds, and rocks—with a Korean cityscape and his own contemporary style. Born in Germany to Korean foreign-service diplomats, Chung lived in many countries growing up. He studied art and animation in the U.S. While teaching at the University of Michigan, Chung maintains a studio in Virginia.

*"Living in the U.S., I'm fascinated with the new ways Korean traditions mix with the global high-tech culture. My childhood memories of Korea are always with me, informing my art and my daily life."*
—Y. David Chung, 2006

## Korean Immigration to the United States
As is the case for the other individual stories in this section of the exhibition, a broader context is provided in photographs – it is the context of Korean immigration to America. A few selected photographs summarize moments in this American story.

The first organized Korean immigration to the United States was in 1903, near the end of the Joseon dynasty. Large groups of Koreans arrived after the Korean War (1953) and throughout

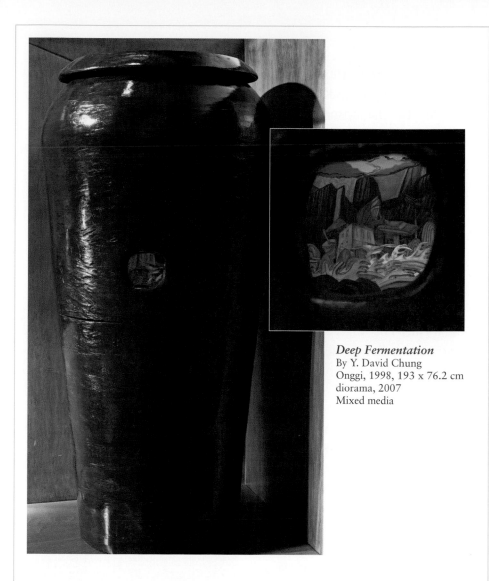

*Deep Fermentation*
By Y. David Chung
Onggi, 1998, 193 x 76.2 cm
diorama, 2007
Mixed media

the late 20th century. At the beginning of the 21st century, an estimated one million Korean Americans live in the U.S.

A photograph in the exhibition from 1906 shows Reverend George Heber Jones visiting Korean immigrants in Hawaii.

Many of the immigrants were recruited by Jones from his church in Korea to work at the plantations.

Another photograph presents Ahn Chang-Ho, one of the most famous early Korean immigrants, who lived in the

United States from 1903 to 1907. He returned to Korea shortly after the Japanese occupation in 1910, to work towards Korean independence.

The importance of the Korean community had grown so much in Los Angeles by 1981 that an area of the city was officially recognized as Koreatown. At a ceremony seen in a third photograph in the exhibition, the former Los Angeles Mayor Thomas Bradley unveils a sign demarcating the area of the city named "Koreatown."

**A Korean-Kazakhstani Artist Mikhail Petrovich Kim** (1923–1990) was born to Korean immigrants in far-eastern Russia, near the border of present-day North Korea. In 1937, at age 14, he and his family were forced by Soviets to move thousands of miles across central Asia to Kazakhstan, which was then part of the Soviet Union.

As a young man Kim studied at a Western style art school. To earn money to continue his studies, he worked on a collective farm for nearly 10 years. At 31, he returned

to his family and eventually began exhibiting his work. He completed several commissions for area buildings before his death. Although he traveled widely after the Soviet regime ended, he always called Kazakhstan his home. His daughter still lives there.

*"At our Kazakhstan home, the family would celebrate Korean-style events like 1st birthday*

*Self portrait*
By Mikhail Petrovich Kim
Oil on canvas, 1960
Image courtesy of Elizaveta Kim

Mikhail Petrovich Kim produced many paintings for Soviet buildings and public spaces, but kept this more introspective self-portrait at his home.

*and 60th birthday. But because my grandparents wanted to help my father master Russian and attend the best school, they spoke only Russian at home."*
—Elizaveta Kim, 2007
(Daughter of Mikhail Kim)

## Koreans in Central Asia

In 1937, the Soviet regime forcibly moved ethnic Koreans who lived in far eastern Russia, fearing they might not be loyal to the Soviet Union. Over 170,000 were deported to Central Asia including Kazakhstan. Fleeing poverty, Koreans had crossed into Russia and Manchuria in search of new lives. After 1937, many Koreans spent years assigned to hard labor on farm collectives. Slowly, they began to adapt to the land, but many of their traditions were lost. Today, many persons of Korean descent are prominent in arts, education, business, and other fields in Kazakhstan, while an Association of Koreans of Kazakhstan encourages the maintenance of Korean traditions.

Other components in the "Korea Beyond Borders" section of the exhibition, at the time of its opening in 2007, relate the story of Korean democracy activist, the Reverend Mun Ik-hwan to larger issues of the division between North Korea and South Korea, and relate the individual story of South Korean golfer Se Ri Pak to the wider involvement of Koreans in international sports.

Reverend **Mun Ik-hwan** (1918-1994) strived for decades to reunite North and South Korea and bring democracy to the peninsula. In 1989 he made an unauthorized visit to North Korea and was arrested upon his return to South Korea. During his lifetime he was imprisoned five times. He was nominated for the Nobel Peace Prize in 1992. South Korea achieved a transition to democracy in 1987. Mun Ik-hwan (pronounced MOON ick-WAHN) studied at the Korea College of Theology (now Hanshin University) and Princeton University. He became an expert on the New Testament and led a team of translators in creating a new Korean translation of the Bible. On the anniversary of his death South Koreans hold lectures and memorial services.

# KOREA BEYOND BORDERS
국경을 넘은 저편의 한국

"At our Kazakhstan home, the family would celebrate Korean-style events like 1st birthday and 60th birthday. But because my grandparents wanted to help my father master Russian and attend the best school, they spoke only Russian at home."
—Elizaveta Kim, 2007
(Daughter of Mikhail Kim)

## Korean Kazakhstani Painter

**Mikhail Petrovich Kim** (1923-1990) was born to Korean immigrants in far-eastern Russia, near the border of present-day North Korea. In 1937, at age 14, he and his family were forced by Soviets to move thousands of miles across central Asia to Kazakhstan.

As a young man Kim studied at a Western-style art school. To earn money to continue his studies, he worked on a collection farm for nearly 10 years. At 31, he returned to his family and eventually began exhibiting his work. He completed several commissions for area buildings before his death. Although he traveled widely after the Soviet regime ended, he always called Kazakhstan his home. His daughter still lives there.

### Koreans in Central Asia
In 1937, the Soviet regime forcibly moved ethnic Koreans who lived in far-eastern Russia, fearing they might not be loyal to the Soviet Union. Over 170,000 were deported to Central Asia including Kazakhstan.

"I have come here to engage in dialogue not with words but with my heart and eyes. No intention to see one side's benefit thus making other's side's loss. I came in search of such words to make all of us the winner as one."
—Mun Ik-hwan, 1989

## Korean Democracy Activist

**Reverend Mun Ik-hwan** (1918-1994) strived for decades to reunite North and South Korea and bring democracy to the peninsula. In 1989 he made an unauthorized visit to North Korea and was arrested upon his return to South Korea. During his lifetime he was imprisoned five times. He was nominated for the Nobel Peace Prize in 1992. South Korea achieved a transition to democracy in 1987.

Mun Ik-hwan (pronounced MOON ick-WAHN) studied at the Korea College of Theology (now Hanshin University) and Princeton University. He became an expert on the New Testament and led a team of translators in creating a new Korean translation of the Bible. On the anniversary of his death South Koreans hold lectures and memorial services.

### A Divided Korea
After over a millennium as a unified nation, Korea became two separate countries at the end of World War II: a Soviet-allied North and a US-allied South. Tensions between the two countries resulted in the Korean War (1950-1953).

**Se Ri Pak** (b. 1977) is a pioneer in Korean sports. At 20 years old she became the youngest player to win the U.S. Women's Open. She went on to win many tournaments and, after ten years as a successful member of the Ladies Professional Golf Association (LPGA), she was inducted into the LPGA Tour and World Golf Halls of Fame in 2007. Pak began training at age 14 with her father, who instilled a disciplined work ethic. Early in her career, she and her family struggled to afford her equipment and fees, and she sometimes took the bus to tournaments. Since then, her success has inspired and influenced young women far beyond her native Korea. In 2007, more than 40 Korean women competed in LPGA events.

*Korea Beyond Borders.*
From left to right: Mikhail Petrovich Kim, Reverend Mun Ik-hwan, and Se Ri Pak.

## Korean Contemporary Art: Past is Present

Within a modest sized space, the Korea Gallery's changing area of "Contemporary Korean Art" presents (at the Gallery's opening) a comparison and contrast between just two artists, the Jeju Island painter Byun Shi-ji and the certified master of a registered "intangible cultural property" art-form, Cho Nam-young. These surprisingly complementary artists present distinctively contrasting examples of how Korea's modern dynamism has found inspiration in Korea's rich past.

### Byun Shi-ji: A Korean Regional Artist with Universal Appeal

Korea's artists excel on the world stage in many creative fields. Many artists draw on their regional or local traditions, incorporating a distinctive identity and visual vocabulary into their work.

Jeju (formerly spelled Cheju) is an oval-shaped island of 1,845 sq km (712.36 sq mi) lying about 150 km (93.21 mi) south of mainland Korea. Jeju (CHEH-joo) holds a unique place in Korean culture. The island's warmer climate and vegetation, and its distinctive houses, stone walls, and carved stone figures called hareubang, help define the region and are easily recognized by Koreans.

**Byun Shi-ji** (b. 1926) was born on Jeju Island, but he grew up in Japan and studied painting there, eventually combining Korean, Japanese, and western styles. When he moved back to Jeju Island in 1975, he began depicting the local landscape. With thick lines he drew the island's distinctive houses, small horses, and stone fences, infusing them with local symbolism. For example, the crows flying above the exhausted artist in *Boisterous Dance* are a sign of hope on Jeju. The aged pine trees in *Leaving Along the Path Like This* are one of Korea's traditional longevity symbols, used here to embody endurance.

*Boisterous Dance*
By Byun Shi-ji
Oil on canvas, 1997, 114 x 164 cm
Loaned by the artist

## Cho Nam-yong: A Master Painter Preserves and Celebrates Tradition

To preserve Korea's diverse cultural traditions, the Korean government and private foundations set up programs to identify and maintain the country's "intangible cultural properties."

Rigorous training or apprenticeship and a system of certification authenticate these traditions. Intangible cultural properties include performances, crafts, rituals and festivals, food, and martial arts among others.

Korean painting traditions classified as intangible cultural properties include Korean folk paintings, the royal "Five Peaks, Sun and Moon" image, and paintings of the ten symbols of longevity.

**Cho Nam-yong** (b. 1946) is a well known exemplar of traditional Korean arts. In

*Ten Symbols of Longevity*
*(Shipjangsaengdo)*
By Cho Nam-yong
Pigment, ink, gold, on mulberry paper with linen
liner, 2007
Loaned by Korea Foundation for Tradition &
Intangible Cultural Properties

2006, she headed both the Korean Folk Art Research Society and the Korean Intangible Culture Promotion Foundation. She is a certified master of particular types of artistic endeavor – including the painting of the traditional "Ten Longevity Symbols." Cho paints with vivid Korean colors and incorporates pigments of pure gold, an element believed to keep away evil spirits. A certified "intangible cultural properties" artist like Cho uses traditional composition, technique, and subject matter but also employs her own style. Cho's deer are much more detailed than those seen in most traditional Korean longevity paintings and she chooses to paint clouds in a more western style.

The ten symbols of longevity— rocks, water, clouds, sun, pine trees, turtles, deer, cranes, bamboo and fungus—were commonly depicted in Korean visual arts of the Joseon dynasty (1392–1910). These and other symbols are also found in Chinese art, but their depiction as a set of ten (called the *shipjangsaengdo*) is uniquely Korean.

# Future Initiatives of the Korea Gallery

The Korea Gallery is designed to be a dynamic exhibition, serving as the "flagship of a fleet" of Korean programming, research, and outreach activities—including publications, films, lectures, and performances. The thematic areas of the exhibition provide an outline of continuing research, and areas for continuing enhancement within the exhibition's framework. For example, the exhibition component surveying contemporary Korean art offers potential space for regular changes and new themes. Topics such as "Korea Beyond Borders" (including Korean American cultural history, and the history of Korean populations in central Asia) are the subject of ongoing cooperative studies at the Smithsonian.

We hope that all those who may enjoy this exhibition will also help sustain the fleet of other activities accompanying it. For example, much research and study remains to be done on the history and cultural context of America's collections from Korea, at the Smithsonian and in other American public and private collections. Many important archival manuscripts remain unpublished, and require study. Our Korea Gallery team also hopes that the public performances, lectures, symposia, and other events comprising the Washington Korea Festival will become a regular occurrence. We hope to continue the initiatives begun with this Korea Gallery, thanks to the help we have been fortunate to receive from many supporters, Smithsonian colleagues, visiting scholars and volunteers.

# SUGGESTED READINGS

*(Note: For ease of locating books, standard Library of Congress citations are provided here. The Library of Congress uses a Korean Romanization system different from that used in the exhibition and in other sections of this book.)*

Adams, Edward Ben. 1987. *Korean folk art & craft*. Seoul, Korea: Seoul International Pub. House.

Brooklyn Museum, and Robert Moes. 1987. *Korean art: from the Brooklyn Museum collection = [Han'guk misul]*. New York: Universe Books.

Chan, Jong-soo, and National Folk Museum of Korea. 2007. *The collection of the National Folk Museum of Korea*. Seoul: Sigong Tech Co., Ltd.

Cho, Chung Hyun. 2004. *From the fire: A survey of contemporary Korean ceramics*. Washington, DC: International Arts & Artists.

Ch'oe, Sun-u. 1979. *5000 years of Korean art*. Seoul: Hyonam Publishing Company.

Chung, Yun Shun Susie. 2005. Seoul, K*orea: its concept of culture and nature in heritage planning*. International Journal of Heritage Studies 11(2):95-111.

George Mason University, Arlington Campus Art Gallery, Myoung-won Kwon, Taemyon Kwon, and Paul Michael Taylor, eds. 2006. *Ah! 560 years of Hangul: A Korean calligraphy exhibition*. Arlington, Virginia: George Mason University, Arlington Campus Art Gallery.

Gidang Contemporary Art Museum of Seogwipo. 2005. *The noble ethos of Korean artist Byun Shi Ji*. Seogwipo, Jejudo: Seogwipo City Gidang Art Museum.

Grant, Bruce K. 1979. *A guide to Korean characters: reading and writing Hangul and Hanja*. 1st ed. Elizabeth, N.J: Hollym International Corp.

Griffing, Robert P. 1968. *The art of the Korean potter: Silla, Koryo, Yi*. New York: Asia Society.

Han, U-gun, and Grafton K. Mintz. 1970. *The history of Korea*. Seoul: Eul-Yoo Publishing Company.

Han'guk Ilbo Muju Ponsa, Miju Hanin Imin 100-chunyon Namgaju Kinyom Saophoe, and Pyong-yong Min. 2004. *Sajin uro ponun Miju Hanin imin 100-yonsa, 1903-2003 = Pictorial book of Korean immigration to the U.S.A.* Los Angeles: Miju Hanin Imin 100-Chunyon Kinyom Saophoe (Namgaju). Han'guk Ilbo Miju Ponsa = Centennial Committee of Korean Immigration to the U.S.A. [and] The Korea Times U.S.A.

Han-Mi Tongp'o Chaedan. 2002. *Miju Hanin imin 100-yonsa = 100-year history of Korean immigration to America: Amerik'an durim ul ch'a*. Los Angeles: Han-Mi Tongp'o Chaedan.

Ho, Tong-hwa, and Han'guk Chasu Pangmulgwan. 2001. Irok'e choun chasu = Voyage to the world of Korean embroidery, Huh, Dong-Hwa collection. Seoul: Han'guk Chasu Pangmulgwan.

Hokkaidoritsu Kindai Bijutsukan, Kokusai Geijutsu Bunka Shinkokai (Japan), Hokkaidoritsu Hakodate Bijutsukan, and Hiroshima Kenritsu Bijutsukan. 2001. *Chosen ocho no bi = Masterpieces of Korean art from the Joseon dynasty, 2001-2002*. Japan: Hokkaido Shinbunsha.

Houchins, Chang-su Cho. 2004. *An ethnography of the Hermit Kingdom: The J.B. Bernadou Korean collection, 1884-1885*. Washington, D.C: Asian Cultural History Program, Smithonian Institution.

Hough, Walter. 1892. The Bernadou, Allen, and Jouy Korean Collections in the U.S. National Museum. *In: The United States National Museum Annual Report for 1891*, pp. 429-488. Washington, D.C.: Smithsonian Institution.

International Cultural Society of Korea. 1989. *Miguk pangmulgwan sojang Han'guk munhwajae = The Korean relics in the United States, Haeoe sojang Han'guk munhwajae*. Seoul: Han'guk Kukche Munhwa Hyophoe.

Kerr, Rose, and Ian Thomas. 1990. *Later Chinese bronzes*. Far Eastern series. London: Bamboo Pub., in association with the Victoria and Albert Museum.

Kim, Eun-young. 2003. Traditional Korean knots. Seoul: Gana Art Publisher.

Kim, Ilpy'ong J. 2004. *Tae Nyuyok Hanin 100-nyonsa = 100 Year history of Korean immigration to the United States 1903-2003*. Seoul: s.n.

Kim, Kumja Paik. 2006. *The art of Korea: Highlights from the collection of San Francisco's Asian Art Museum*. 1st ed. San Francisco, Calif.: Asian Art Museum.

Kim, Kumja Paik, Asian Art Museum - Chong-Moon Lee Center for Asian Art and Culture, Kungnip Chungang Pangmulgwan (Korea), and Nara Kokuritsu Hakubutsukan. 2003. *Goryeo dynasty: Korea's age of enlightenment, 918-1392*. San Francisco: Asian Art Museum - Chong-Moon Lee Center for Asian Art and Culture in cooperation with the National Museum of Korea and the Nara National Munseum.

Kim, Kumja Paik, and Tong-hwa Ho. 1995. *Profusion of color: Korean costumes & wrapping cloths of the Choson Dynasty*. San Francisco; Seoul: Asian Art Museum of San Francisco; Museum of Korean Embroidery.

Kim, Nam-choon. 2005. *Ecological restoration and revegetation works in Korea*. Landscape and Ecological Engineering 1:77-83.

Kim, Ockrang, Sukman Jang, and Charlotte Horlyck. 2007. *Korean funerary figures: Companions for the journey to the Other World*. N. L. [in English]: Ockrang Cultural Foundation.

Kim, Wonyong, Roderick Whitfield, and Youngsook Pak. 1986. *Korean Art Treasures*. Seoul: Yekyong Publications Co.

Knez, Eugene I. 1997. *The modernization of three Korean villages, 1951-1981 an illustrated study of a people and their material culture, Smithsonian contributions to anthropology*. Washington, D.C: Smithsonian Institution Press.

Korea (South), and Munhwajaech`ong. 2006. *Important intangible cultural heritage*. Daejeon: Cultural Heritage Administration.

Korea National Tourism Organization. 2007. *Korean cultural insights*. Seoul: Korea National Tourism Organization.

Korean Art Crafts Exhibition, Korean Craft Promotion Foundation, Ministry of Culture & Tourism (Korea), and Embassy of the Republic of Korea in U.S.A. 2002. *Beauty of traditional Korean wedding culture*. Seoul: Korean Craft Promotion Foundation.

Lawton, Thomas, and Linda Merrill. 1993. Freer: a legacy in art. Washington, D.C.; New York: Smithsonian Institution, in association with H.N. Abrams.

Lawton, Thomas, Fu Shen, Glenn D. Lowry, Ann Yonemura, and Milo Beach. 1987. *The inaugural gift: Asian art in the Arthur M. Sackler Gallery*. Washington, D.C.: Arthur M. Sackler Gallery.

Moes, Robert, International Exhibitions Foundation, and Korean Overseas Information Service. 1983. *Auspicious spirits: Korean folk paintings and related objects.* Washington, D.C: The Foundation.

National Academy of the Korean Language. 2002. *An illustrated guide to Korean culture 233 traditional key words.* Seoul: Hakgojae.

National Folk Museum of Korea. 1995. *Kundae paengnyon minsok p`ungmul : kwangbok 50-chunyon kinyom t`ukpyolchon = Reflection on the Recent 100 Years Time: changes in Korean custom and life.* Seoul: Kungnip Minsok Pangmulgwan [=National Folk Museum of Korea].

———. 2003. *The elegance and beauty of the life of the Yangban in the Joseon dynasty.* Seoul: National Folk Museum of Korea.

———. 2004. *Namu wa chongi, Han`guk ui chont`ong kongye = Wood and paper in Korean traditional crafts.* Seoul: Kungnip Minsok Pangmulgwan.

———. 2005. *Minhwa wa jangsik byeongpung = Korean folk painting and screens, Minsok umul ihae [= "The Understanding of Folk Artifacts"].* Seoul: Gungnip minsok bangmulgwan.

Sayers, Robert, and Ralph Rinzler. 1987. *The Korean onggi potter.* Washington, D.C.: Smithsonian Institution Press.

Sigong Tech, and Korea Visuals. 2002. *Korean cultural heritage: Seen through pictures and names.* South Korea: Sigong Tech; Korea Visuals.

Taylor, Paul Michael. 2003. *Snapshots from A Korean American Century.* KoreAm Journal 14(5):50-54 (May 2003).

Taylor, Paul Michael, Chang-su Houchins, Hui-su Kim, Hanguk Kukche Kyoryu Chaedan, Smithsonian Institution., Korea (South), Taesagwan (U.S.), and Washington Korea Festival (2007), eds. 2007. *Washington Korea Festival 2007: celebrating the opening of the Smithsonian's new Korea Gallery, May-June 2007.* Washington, D.C.: Korea Foundation.

The Center for Information on Korean Culture, and The Academy of Korean Studies. 2005. *Korea today.* Seoul: The Academy of Korean Studies.

The Korean Society of Calligraphic Arts, UCLA, and Los Angeles Korean Cultural Center. 2006. *Beauty of Hangul calligraphy in USA.* Los Angeles: The Korean Society of Calligraphic Arts, UCLA [and] Korean Cultural Center, Los Angeles.

White, Julia M. , and Huh Dong- hwa. 2003. *Wrappings of happiness: A traditional Korean art form.* Hawaii; Seoul: Honolulu Academy of Arts; Museum of Korean Embroidery.

Whitfield, Roderick. 2004. *Dictionary of Korean art and archaeology.* Elizabeth, New Jersey; Seoul: Hollym.

Yi, Ki-baek. 1984. *A new history of Korea.* Seoul: Ilchokak.

Yi, Song-mi. 2002. *Fragrance, elegance, and virtue Korean women in traditional arts and humanities.* Seoul: Daewonsa.

Yun, Yong-i, and Regina Krahl. 2006. *Korean art from the Gompertz and other collections in the Fitzwilliam Museum: a complete catalogue.* Cambridge: Cambridge University Press.

Yunesuk`o Han'guk Wiwonhoe. 1983. *The Korean language.* Seoul: Si-sa-yong-o-sa Publishers; Pace International Research.

# CREDITS

## Photos by:

**Smithsonian Institution, Asian Cultural History Program staff (2007-2008):** pp. 6, 9, 16, 29, 40, 76, 82, 83, 85 (bottom), 90-91, 94 (bottom)

**Smithsonian Institution, Chip Clark:** front cover, pp. 1, 14, 30-31, 34, 38-39, 41, 52, 53 (bottom), 56, 72, 73, 84, 85 (top), 94 (top three photos), 96, 97 (top)

**Smithsonian Institution, James Di Loreto:** pp. 10, 42, 44-45, 46, 47, 48, 50-51, 53 (top), 54-55, 59, 60-61, 62, 63, 65, 66, 68-69, 70, 71, 74, 77, 78, 79, 88-89, 101, back cover

**Smithsonian Institution, Donald Hurlbert:** pp. 4-5, 12-13

**Smithsonian Institution, John Steiner:** pp. 45 (bottom), 64, 104-105

**Smithsonian Institution, Randy S. Tims:** p. 26

**Kim Sungyun:** p. 80

**Lee Young Hee Museum:** pp. 92-93

**Byun, Joung Hun:** p. 98, 107

**Foundation for Traditional & Intangible Cultural Properties:** p. 108-109

*(Credit information for archival photographs is listed in captions.)*

# Acknowledgements

This book was produced by the Asian Cultural History Program (Gregory P. Shook, Program Manager), in conjunction with the Korea Gallery, an exhibition co-curated by Paul Michael Taylor and Chang-su Cho Houchins (Asian Cultural History Program, National Museum of Natural History, Smithsonian Institution).

The Korea Gallery and its associated activities were made possible by the generous sponsorship of **The Korea Foundation**, with additional support from **GK Power** and **Korean Air**, and from many other donors and sponsors, including: **Byun, Joung-hun, Pung Yoon (Minn) Chang, Gangjin City (Korea), Gwangju City (Korea), Jeonju City (Korea), KI Graphics, Mookjae Kwon Myoung-won, Lee Young Hee Museum, LG Electronics, Brian and Moon O'Connor, Yong In University, and Sam-kyun Yoon**. Many thanks are also due to the Embassy of the Republic of Korea (Washington, D.C.) and to the National Folk Museum of Korea; and special thanks for community support to the **Korean Heritage Foundation** (Arlington, Virginia).

This Guide to the Korea Gallery has been made possible by Korea Gallery exhibition financial support from **GK Power,** with special thanks to Mr. Seo Kyoung-duk and Mr. Hyek Chen. The initial book photographic and design coordination was done by Dong-hyok So (Smithsonian Institution). The authors especially wish to thank Sooki Moon (of KI Graphics) for designing the book, with the help of Erin Byun. The script (or text) used in the exhibition itself was developed with the help of the entire exhibition development team, and forms the basis for the object descriptions in the exhibition and in this book.

The exhibition's co-curators (Paul Michael Taylor and Chang-su Cho Houchins) worked closely with the other members of the Korea Gallery exhibit development team: Junko Chinen (Project Manager), Margery Gordon (Exhibit Educator), Sarah Grusin (Exhibit Scriptwriter/Editor), Andrew Pekarik (Content Advisor, from the Smithsonian's Office of Policy and Analysis), Michel D. Lee (Researcher), this book's co-author Christopher Lotis (Researcher/Publications Director), Meg Rivers (Project Assistant), the designers at the exhibition's design firm Reich & Petch, and our Visiting Museum Professionals from the National Folk Museum of Korea, Lee Tae-hee and Kim Hee-soo. The exhibition's external content reviewers were Prof. Young-key Kim-Renaud of The George Washington University, and Dr. Robert Sayers.

Many other Smithsonian colleagues, in addition to the development team, helped to develop and produce the exhibition. Staff members from numerous departments and offices helped, including (using the names from 2007, prior to a reorganization of some offices) the Office of Exhibits, Office of Education, Office of Development and Public Affairs, Office of the Registrar, Office of Imaging and Photographic Services, the Department of Anthropology, and the Office of the Director, all within the National Museum of Natural History. Colleagues from many other parts of the Smithsonian also helped, including the Freer Gallery of Art and the Arthur M. Sackler Gallery, the Smithsonian Institution Libraries, the Office of Policy and Analysis, Office of International Relations, Office of Protection Services, and others. We thank all the dedicated Smithsonian staff, docents, volunteers, and many others who helped make this exhibition possible.